THE RIVER IS RISING

THE RIVER IS RISING

Patricia Jabbeh Wesley

Autumn House Press

PITTSBURGH

"Autumn House" and "Autumn House Press" are registered trademarks
owned by Autumn House Press, a nonprofit corporation whose mission
is the publication and promotion of poetry and other fine literature.

Autumn House Press Staff
Executive Editor and Founder: Michael Simms
Executive Director: Richard St. John
Community Outreach Director: Michael Wurster
Co-Director: Eva-Maria Simms
Fiction Editor: Sharon Dilworth
Special Projects Coordinator: Joshua Storey
Associate Editors: Anna Catone, Laurie Mansell Reich
Editorial Consultant: Ziggy Edwards
Media Consultant: Jan Beatty
Tech Crew Chief: Michael Milberger
Intern: Laura Crawford

ISBN: 978-1-932870-18-3
Library of Congress Control Number: 2007925339

This book is for the women in my life

Sharon Sue Denk, my friend, sister, and hero—
you taught me something about being a woman,
and showed me how to dry my tears those first
few months in your home.

My two daughters—
Besie-Nyesuah and *Ade-Juah Wesley*,
two people who are becoming strong women

The tens of thousands of *Liberian women* who survived—
and to the memory of the tens of thousands who
did not survive to tell their own stories.

A Memorial for Herbert Scott

My deepest gratitude and love to Herb Scott
and to the memory of the person he was—
poet, publisher, father-teacher-friend-mentor,
lover of poetry and lover of students.
...Death can take only the body from us,
but you continue to live in us and in the poetry
you so easily inspired in us.

Folks like you never really die, you know....

Acknowledgments

I am grateful to my friends, family, and fellow poets in the United States, Africa and around the world who have supported and encouraged me over the years. I am particularly grateful to Dr. Robert H. Brown of the United Kingdom, Liberian writer, teacher, and friend, who continues to be a great inspiration and support to me. I am also grateful to Althea Romeo Mark of Switzerland, my former teacher and friend who believed in me thirty years ago, and told me that I could be a poet. Thanks also to my writing friends out there: Gbanabom Hallowell, Annaird Naxela, Stephanie Horton, and many others. I am especially grateful for my WMU bunch: Lydia Melvin, Beth Martinelli, Adela Najarro, Becky Beech. To my dear Cynthia Hogue, I say hey, girl, thanks for being a sister. I am also grateful to my dear friends, Allison Joseph and Jon Tribble for everything under the sun. And to Michael Simms and his entire staff, I say thanks for all you do. Finally, I am grateful to my dear sweet husband, Mlen-Too Wesley, who is always there.

I would also like to thank the editors of the following journals or magazines in which some of the poems in this book or excerpts have appeared or are forthcoming:

The American Journal of Nursing (AJN): "All Dirges Have Ceased"

Newsday Magazine, Long Island: "In The Ruined City: A Poem for Monrovia"

Crab Orchard Review: "Until The Plane Drops," "What The Land Carver Said From the Sky," "Ruined Trails," and "Coming Home: For Besie-Nyesuah"

Penn State Research Magazine: "Monrovia Revisited," and "The Women In My Family"

The Driftwood: "At Point Loma," and "Women at the Tomb"

Transition Magazine: "Strange Woman" and "City"

Private International Review: "City" and "The Morning After: An Elegy"

Alehouse Press: "Poem Written from a Single Snapshot"

Pittsburgh City Paper: "One of These Days, We Should Give Her a Medal"

Sea Breeze Journal of Contemporary Liberian Writings: "Monrovia Revisited," All Dirges Have Ceased," "In the Ruined City: A Poem for Monrovia," and "The River Is Rising"

Common Wealth: Contemporary Poets on Pennsylvania: "This Hill Will Get You There"

The Autumn House Poetry Series

Contents

III   UMBILICAL CORDS

IV WOMAN

To Set Everything Right

Legend keeps the story of the Grebo women
who were going to wash all that salt out of the Atlantic.
Villagers from all over Grebo country spent years
boiling buckets of salt water away—
All that arrogance coming from women,
women, who were just women—
Women, wanting to set the ocean
right once and for all?

They decided to end all that flapping and foaming,
the way a man foams when a woman
stands her ground. Women came down
from Yederobo, Gbanmakeh, Tugbakeh, Manolu,
Gedetaabo, Gbanelu, Taakeh, Galloway...
women, their lappas flying in the salty breeze,
down the Cape in Gbanelu.
And when the men saw all this fussing,
they laughed, and thought of ways to put
all that feminism to rest.

If they came down from all these towns,
what then would they do with their husbands?
What would they put in their husbands'
bowls for feed? Fix them to drink?
To wash with?—Women, like ants,
washing away buckets and pails of salt
day after day, month after month,
forgetting to birth babies all those years,
just washing out the salty ocean,
but it was no use—oh how the washing

of the Atlantic kept their babies from
growing up, kept their husbands from farming,
from eating, from laughing,
kept their sons from coming out to be men...
—Just one woman dashed her pail away

1

and picked up her baby, and every woman followed...
to feed the men, to cook that spicy
palm butter that can put a man to sleep,
to smoke tabadu tender and smelly,
so the bone cracks under a man's teeth,
without cracking a tooth...

THOSE WHO SURVIVED

We are characters now other than before
The war began, the stay-at-home unsettled
By taxes and rumor, the looter for office
And wares, fearful everyday the owners may return

from "The Casualties"
John Pepper Clark Bekederemo

Lamentation After Fourteen Years

If you can sit beside the river long enough,
the tide will come in. You'll be there
for the river's rising—that urgent leaping
only a river can make.
You'll see how the coming tide departs,
leaving behind herring, catfish, *gbuga*,
snappers, where river meets swamp,
where swamp meets land, meeting you.

You'll see the crab or fish or lobsters or clams,
forgotten in the river's rush back to sea.
The poor used to wait on Monrovia's beaches
with bowls or baskets for the fishermen at sea.
Give-away catch can now feed a household.
Today we wait with straw baskets
and buckets, long lines,
we wait, all over the world, we wait;

not for *gbuga* fish or snails, not for the river's
refuse or the fisherman's *dash*—
Instead, we wait for peace, days of quiet,
ocean nights. They say, "if you set your eye
on the moon, you can see right through it."
So I clip away tree branches around my house,
from my front way, so when night finally
comes, I can sit under the sky
and watch the moon come home.

We do not long for yams or rice or oil. We do not
long for clothes or beds or babies; we sigh, not
for lack of tears or lack of laughter. We sit here,
my family and I, reliving the war—Charles Taylor's
cruel warfare haunts us like weeds left so long,
they eat up the yard. We sit here, God,
and we say, give us peace. We ask for

those quiet nights where only the Atlantic's
waves can roar. After so many years,
we long only for the end of war—
not for bread or beef; not for gin or rice,
not for roads or guns, not for street lights—
the sun comes out, and we say, God,
just give us the moon, the big blue moon.

This Hill Will Get You There

This is the beginning of country.
The roads bend sideways as though
they themselves could fall off these
winding cliffs. Where trees lean and houses
bend, cattle uphill in some far-away field
seem to all lean sideways, eating sideways.
But this hill will get you there.
Although the ground winds up and down
steep green that seems to take you
to the end of earth. Before you reach
Pittsburgh, you will wonder
if this trip was worth it after all.

There is no level ground up here—
no plains, no cornfields, no flat landscape
so your eye can reach the end of earth.
There is no way of knowing tomorrow,
of knowing sky from below.
If you believe in sky, take it, it is blue
and beautiful, and at times, there is no
dividing line between where the trees
end and where sky begins.

I hold my breath as we wind up
another hill and up another hill until
there is no breath left in me.
This is what I sold myself to—
this is what I get for giving up the lakes'
surfing in Michigan, the fresh waters
of Michigan that stretch endless,
and yet wild as the ocean knows

strength. This is what I get, having
abandoned the Atlantic, where as a child
I used to run wild upon Monrovia's
salty beaches. There is no salt here, no
fresh water, no foaming waves, and yet
these green hills steal my heart.
These never-ending hills that sigh deep
just before the day turns to twilight.

At Galilee

For Pastor J. Louis Felton, at Galilee

The women come in, wearing hats spread out
in the air like the wings of a jumbo jet.

Immaculate dresses and coat suits,
white stockings and needle heels even though

they're long past fifty. And when they stand
and shout, "Hallelujah," oh, my, you

will break your knee just standing and looking.
Everything 'bout them sparkles

and jingles even though they aren't even rich.
At Galilee, where all the women know

how to polish brown cheeks, darken around
their eyelids till they shine like gold.

The men wear long coats and necklaces,
bracelets and shirts that hang down like curtains.

I say, girl, the men at Galilee will even wear
earrings, jerry-curl, fine black hair or shave

their hair almost bald. Just wait 'til someone
gets the Holy Ghost, and begins to jump up

and down, and the drums go pounding, ushers
rush with fans and tissues, and the women

in their white suits who are trained
in Mouth to Mouth resuscitation, encircle

the jumping, Holy-Ghost-filled woman
or man, in case of a heart attack. I sit back

and watch my people after four hundred years,
they still holler and dance, dress-up, jump

and shout like the people back in Mama's
Church in Monrovia. In Mama's church,

you can sit all day singing and shouting
and jumping, the hot sun melting tarred

roofs, while we sing and shout 'til Jesus
himself gets out of his Heavenly seat,

and says "oh yes." Instead of hats, the women
at the Church of God in Christ wear Choko

or head-ties that rise in the air or spread like
the wings of a big plane, and no one can see

the Pastor who is also jumping and shouting
on stage the way my Pastor does here

at Galilee. The women wear lipstick and brown
their cheeks too, wear high-heeled shoes

just like we do at Galilee. People cry and scream
'til the roof shakes above our heads too,

at Mama's church, and ushers rush to wipe
the Holy-Ghost-filled worshippers' sweaty

brows, and everyone shouts "Hallelujah!"

The River Is Rising

a song for Liberian women

The river is rising, and this is not a flood.
After years of drought, the ground, hardened

and caked in blood, in dry places, here we are, today.

River banks are swelling with the incoming tide,
coming in from the Atlantic just beyond the ridge

of rolling hills and rocks in Monrovia.

Finally, here we stand at the banks!
Finally, here we are, see how swiftly

the tide rushes in to fill the land with salt.

Fish and crabs and the huge clams and shrimp—
all the river's creatures are coming in with the tide.

The river is rising, but this is not a flood.

Do not let your eye wander away from this scene.
Yes, all the bones below the Mesurado or the St. Paul

or Sinoe or the Loffa River will be brought up
to land so all the overwhelming questions
can once more overwhelm us.

But they are bringing in our lost sister
on a high stool, and there she stands, waving at those

who in refusing to die, simply refused to die.

This is not a song for Ellen alone. This is a song
for Mapue and Tenneh and all the Ellens there are.

This is a song for Kimah and Musu and Massa.

This is for Nyeneplue and Nyenoweh, for Kou and Glayee
and Korto, for the once solitary woman of war.

This is a song so Wani will also dance.

This is a song for that small girl child who came out
just this morning. They are still seeking a name

to call her—a river name, a name from the water
and from the fire too. That solitary mother in flight

will no longer birth her child by the roadside
where shells were her baby's first bed.

Let the womb quiver!
Let church bells jingle!
Let hundreds of drums pound, Klan-klan-teh!
Let men bring out old trumpets
so the wind will take flight!

Let that small pepper bird on the tree branch
cry and sing no more the solitary song.

Let the Mesurado rise behind my home or what was
my home or still is or maybe, maybe, who cares?

The river is rising, but this is not a flood.

Let no man stand between us
and the river again!

In Case of Water Landing

To fly into Michigan, you must first fly over Michigan.
Wet, penetrating, surfing, unreliable as any lake can be.

Anything insoluble will demand another route.
At the outskirts of what looks like any city, Chicago

stands, defiant, edgy and biting. The heavy musky sky
with skyscrapers at the edge of a world on edge.

Passengers must sit stiff until land comes in sight,
after Chicago fades into sky and the lake recedes into

itself, Michigan emerges at last, a state, no longer
a body of water. I love the feeling of staying afloat,

but landing is such a good thing. The feet were made
to dwell on solid ground. Imagine Noah docking

on water after The Flood, leading hundreds of animals
afloat on a cushion from beneath his Ark's seat. But Noah

would not dock until he'd found land, knowing how
dependable only land is, something water is forever

seeking to know. On my flight, the attendant is teaching
us how to stay alive in a crash, how to stay afloat, how

to pull out the cushion from beneath our legs, our hands
holding on tightly to the air mask, the other hand pulling

out the cushion. And if you are seated at the exit, you will
need a third hand to open the heavy metal door and lead

everyone onto air. The cushion will be good for water
landing, for the air bubbles that ride upon wet waves.

Just hang on to the cushion and the mask and then let go
of the seat belt because the plane is now jerking, crashing,

exploding, in search of water. Remember, the cushion is still
being held by your trembling other hand you never really had.

The cushion, she says, is great for flotation, a device
originally meant for floating during a plane crash until

someone placed it beneath your large bottom to float on
while the plane still floats on air. Any time one needs

a cushion to float on in case of water landing, it is
no landing at all. Have you ever seen a plane crash survivor

who landed on water and got out floating on a flotation
device from beneath an airplane's seat? I love the earth,

its cruel solidity of crushed surfaces, iron rocks, dust,
sand and muck. Trees do not have to make themselves felt

since they are always called trees. But I see, our plane
has crossed Lake Michigan into Michigan, at last.

After Deer Season

After deer season, a deer trots across my lawn
with her entire family. Survivors, I call them,
survivors, while my nine-year-old hollers
for everyone to see our new neighbors,
the deer family. The woman next door
has already warned us that there will be bears
and deer and squirrels and everything else
that has a claim to our yard. That when
the bears come through on a summer evening,
we should be indoors. I was not told before
I bought this house and the lawn and the trees
in the sloping hills in my backyard. I know
how to share my home with the mouse
or the black ant and the spiders and, sometimes,
the bees—and their entire extended friends.
They say you walk backwards when you see
a bear, backwards until you stumble upon a rock
and fall. Backwards even though this is your house.
Last night on the evening news a woman
met her bear neighbor for the first time as she
strolled into her garage—a bear and the house
owner wrestling. These facts should be
disclosed at the Title office, I'd say.

Bringing Closure

Closure is such a final thing—the needle in the arm,
one last word or no last word at all, a death chamber

where the supposed convict lies waiting so the poison
will descend or ascend to the heart, a final beat,

and then sleep, that eternal thing none of us living
has ever seen. In California, today, a man is being

put to death, but outside, his supporters wait; candles,
flames, anger—the cold chill of death and life,

and a country that waits for all the arguments to die
or live on. The victim's mother will see closure today,

they say, and move on after the murderer or the supposed
murderer is laid to rest with her son, side by side.

Death is such an ironic thing to know. To know death
is to know rot, hush, the lack of pain. It is 3 a.m.

in Pennsylvania. Time, so deceptive, and arbitrary
and imperfect. Around the world, we all wait, for

the executioner's poke into vein, blood meeting poison.
We are such civilized people, I'd say, dishing out death

in small poking needles. The newsmen tell us they
cannot find his vein. The awkwardness of asking the one

awaiting death to find his own vein so they can murder
him too—the executioner's awkward fingers, the knowing

fingers—afraid of both the man and the art of killing the man.
I hate death. I hate the dying, the ugly process of dying,

the ritual of murder. So I too keep vigil on my carpet.
Tomorrow, I'll tell my eleven-year-old daughter how

we have all murdered another human being. An eye
for an eye, so far away from my bedroom of dim lights,

a comforter or two, the surrounding hills in close view.
There is always a mountain here in Pennsylvania,

always that looming presence of life and death and the
far away feeling of the valley below, of being so far away

from home. There is no closure, I see, after the poison
has reached the heart, and the accused, stretched out, finally.

The victim's mother begins to weep all over again—
as if this were just the beginning of the dying.

One of These Days, We Should Give Her a Medal

A woman who has turned gray in the air—
the airline stewardess down the aisles,
fitting her new body between tight rows
that weren't meant for her.
After nine eleven, they went back
into the years

for those who know the air—those who once
breathed in the sky through thin nostril passages—
those with bomb-sniffing tubes in their heads
so we can sit safe on air.
I place my rough hands in my lap
and swallow.

All the tiny girls with their soft faces have been
replaced by the strong ones—
those who know us so well, they are as
reliable as water down
the throat of a canal.

You have to see her lifting those arms,
her now frail flesh, serious eyes, and voice.
She'd stood on air so many
years, it became solid ground
beneath her large feet.

One of these days, we should give her
a medal. We should all line up beside
the plane upon landing, and give
her the Bronze Star for not
letting us drown
in the Atlantic.

In Michigan

In Michigan, we plant flowers in June after snow
finally gives in to spring. Road repair crews pull

out bulldozers and set up roadblocks along highways.
Flowers are sure to bloom in July—daffodils, roses,

lilies, carnations, violets—imagine their colorful beauty.
You have to see the trees when they bloom—trees

covered with pink, yellow, purple butterfly petals,
flowers snapping at the world. All the old women

and old men gather tools for front and back yards then.
When you are old, this is what you'll do, an old

woman told me one day. Of all the things in life,
this is what I'll do? I'll wait for flowers to bloom,

and then I'll dig and shovel, making way so spring
presses its fickle beauty onto leaves and stems?

After all of this, then comes August, August all over
again, and the cold winds return from the lakes—

from Michigan, Huron, Erie—and we begin to bundle
up in preparation for indoors. The ice returns in patches,

then the snow. Old women can then set aside their
gardens and shovels, fly away to warmer places where

others know what the sunlight really is. We who cannot
leave, sit indoors and wait—endlessly, for that whiteness

that is beautiful only when seen from the other side
of the window, from the other side of the issue.

Memories

When the trees give away their leaves
so winter will come, it's like a brushfire.
Trees stand in their bare bones, naked; twigs, sticking out,
and on the ground, little white icicles gather overnight
as if winter will not come again.

On Byron Center's farm streets, you can
almost hear the echo of your own scream.
Byron Center holds up all the world's silence this
time of year. In the supermarket's aisle, a Dutch woman
is bent over, picking up a can of stewed beef,

a jar of bouillon cubes, a smile for the stranger girl
who's learning her way in an all-Dutch town. It is her accent
and her talk of pigs-in-blanket and Dutch apple pies that
turn my heart as I giggle to hear her World War II story
all over again in between shelves of food
in the supermarket's aisle.

She's talking of years ago when she,
arriving in America, like me, one bundle of clothing,
her breath of air and hoping like me, just for one more day.
In between her Dutch on English,
I can see all the trees in Byron being felled for cattle
and corn and children and church,

and then I come to stand here and laugh here,
and cry here about my own war, clinging to
my own past and a war still being fought at home.
My 80-year-old Dutch ally clings to a can
of stewed beef, to children, grandchildren,
great-grandchildren, and memories.

Shakespeare 550

Shakespeare stalks my basement corridors, in
between dusty pages, his long gray beard and tiny

spectacles, calling out to Hamlet to put away
the sword. Hamlet, who will not let Claudius alone.

My professor teaches Shakespeare the way
only Macbeth could have taught Shakespeare.

She weeps when she teaches King Lear and his
good-for-nothing daughters. King Lear, weeping

in the storm, King Lear giving away his fortune
before his death. My professor wipes her large,

blue eyes when she remembers King Lear.
I pity my professor who weeps for King Lear.

My professor who loves the storm and the rain
and King Lear, caught in the rain. She was

Shakespeare's lover when he wrote Macbeth,
the two of them, sitting beside the fireplace,

editing Macbeth. She loves Macbeth who plots
his own death at midnight, when the fireplace

is finally cold, and only witches can prowl dark
hallways while a dagger strikes home. My professor

envies Macbeth who stalks his own hallways
with a dagger. Macbeth who can kill his enemies

so easily. Everyone should be able to kill their enemies
with a dagger. Everyone should be able to wash their

hands clean at the end of a class. I am afraid of my
professor's eyes, her organized smile. After so long,

I can still see my professor standing under the oak tree
on my block, talking with the weeping king who

reminds her of her dead father and the snow
falling lightly outside. Her cold hands and feet,

her cold white tears. Today my professor killed
Shakespeare and Othello and Macbeth and Hamlet

and Ophelia, and all the huge books on my table.
Her own Othello with his brute face and hands.

Othello with an inflamed face, his foaming mouth.
Death is an angry God in Shakespeare, I'd say.

When my professor discusses Othello, students
sit mute, staring up at her telling us that Othello

is a brute pagan who murders Desdemona, his wife.
If he had killed a Moor like himself, it wouldn't

have been murder, she says. She wants to put Othello
to death, but Othello is already dead, like Macbeth,

like Hamlet and Claudius, all of them, dead, like
King Lear, like Shakespeare. I should have told her

to let Othello die, to let Shakespeare die the way
he massacred all those fine people. Shakespeare,

who knew how to murder with the sword.
Let the dead bury the dead, I should have said.

Four Tibetan Monks on a Wall at the Arts Council

The monastery from where these monks came
was built in 1447, before World War I, before

Hitler came spitting out words like bullets
even though words are true bullets; before there

was even a gun. Before the world arrived at its
present state with too many swords pointed

at frail people. Only the first Dalai Lama will tell
you how these monks came to be, caught in

a whirlwind in a world that has forgotten how
to give back freedom to those whose freedoms

we've stolen. All over the world these monks
roam, in search of home, in search of the stream

where Buddha first learned to chant songs about
the lost peoples in the lost land. Here they are,

now, looking for Buddha whose limbs still tie
them all to China. These monks want to go back

home where the hills used to touch the skies.
Four monks at a cross-limb in history, forgotten

people, forgotten songs, where the artist leaves
them vulnerable like charred pieces of unburned

portions of a really-burnt house, our eyes wide
and staring. Forgotten dreams—as though all

the hearers of your one song are deaf men.
Abandoned monks, left here so an artist can know

abandonment, so an oil painting will breathe
small air. We are making new exiles so more

paintings will live. Tomorrow, I will go down
and visit your mute selves, dear monks; your

mute shrines where the poor artist wishes to open
me up to color and beauty, to a hundred more

questions where prayer is not just for the knees to do.
Poor artist, poor painter, poor poet, I can hear

the chant of one lost monk in a town where so many
are trying to be found. On the streets, the cars go

slow, downtown Kalamazoo, a church bell hums soft
melody, lost monks, captive people, rise up out of

this painting and flee before the sun's eternal eclipse.

Tomorrow We Will Go Out into the Streets

At night just before the cricket goes to sleep,
I gather myself like a woman with large arms,
like a woman with wings, like a woman
with all the world beneath her large foot.
The children are sleeping now, but my clock
battery allows it to tick on into the next day,
refusing to be captured by sleep.

Tomorrow, we will go out into the streets
and gather the day's air into nostrils.
Tomorrow we will go out into the city
and gather dust for the coming years.
We will go into church and sing
about all the things we have never done,
about meeting God in Heaven someday,
and Pastor will shout as if he really means
business, and the woman next to me will
weep and scramble around for a napkin
all over again, weeping about the sins she's
planning to commit tomorrow,
and I will be beside myself all over again.

At dawn, everyone goes—all over again,
we go. This world of people coming
and going, and the taxi driver whose only
mission is to see people go. On 7th Avenue
in Manhattan, people get up and go, and yet
no one stops to stare at the day. On 7th Avenue
in Manhattan, the boy from Senegal is shouting
in Wolof at another boy from Senegal,
and I stand there and stare.

In the dark, people pass in dark winter coats,
the boy from Senegal and his friends from
Senegal, and I stand here, but they will not
know that I have also left home, deserted
my continent just like them. In this world,
a woman gets up and gets married,
and the husband dies, and she marries another
who dies, and she marries another who dies.
Three men, slipping through the hands
of a single woman, men going and coming
through one woman's fingers just like that.

Blessed Are the Sinful for They Shall See God

Blessed are the sinful, for they shall see God
in his plainness without makeup,
for he has no need to be God to them.
They are devils and villains, man-mongers and woman-mongers,
whores and prostitutes, vampires and robbers.
Baby killers and smokers of vampires,
who shall stand before the throne without flip-flops or sandals,
and he shall look at them without blinking or winking
or pretending that they are even righteous.
Blessed are sinners who come into a swinging door
singing Amazing Grace.
For what use is grace without anyone to grace
and what use is sin without a song?
I will be there, waiting to see what God has to say
to people like all of us, one bag
of iron rocks and sin—plain simple sin.
They shall be as blessed as the ocean waves
after twilight—as sinful as the righteous.

Taking Possession

Every time you buy a new home, you're afraid of taking
possession of another person's house. There are

overwhelming discoveries when you enter the doorway,
when you enter the kitchen. All the hours of paper-signing,

done, and now, the feeling of having conquered America,
having arrived, a stranger just to own a house you didn't build.

In the door, you discover all the missing bolts, the creaking
things any house knows how to hide, the windowpane that

was broken even though it was not put on display at showings.
All the trimmings that came with the house fail you in an

attempt to tell you, this is not your home. Numerous ghosts
of past owners lurk in dark places, ghosts of those who

would have bought the house, should have bought it, may
have, could have, if the bank had been only a bit kinder.

All these faces will wake up with you each morning. You are
the ex-lover, wanting to possess again that old house with

all its bolts where you left them, where you felt at home on
familiar territory, where the windows you broke understand

how totally kind you are, and the neighbors already know
your faults, and still like you or dislike you. There, the territory

is flat and dependable, a place where no one can size you up
all over again. Now, you're being possessed by old ghosts, by

dead people's failed visions, and here you are, standing on
new ground, in another town that looks like another country.

At Point Loma

At Point Loma, a student may dip a toe or two in
the ocean, in between classrooms and teachers, in

between falling in and out of love, between the pages
of a book's silence. On a fast day, the windy air, misty,

salty, so much beauty for the eyes, and I'd say, what a life!
In my small Pennsylvania town, old railroad tracks

still wind their way around Altoona, old steel country,
rusting away from lack of use, the green mountains,

rising like clumps of dirt mounds. Altoona, where
some will never understand how a student can learn

anything sitting on a beach. But in San Diego, the
hotel suite, where my kind hosts have lavished this

undeserved luxury upon me, a suite that hangs over
the bay, the lovely balcony frightens me though.

What if I slip and fall into this old bay where a man
rises out of his boat at dawn as if he were a fish.

His wheelbarrow, squeaking with things he is hauling
on to his boat on the bay. There are so many boats,

the water has no air to breathe; the air has no water
to drink. There is so much in this life to live for,

and yet my boat neighbors have chosen to live on
the water, not on the shoreline, on the sand, or on

the bare cliffs where Point Loma University, so
blessed, sits along the peaceful shoreline as if waiting

for God. This is the sort of place that follows
the traveler around forever, like the old stories Iyeeh

told me in Dolokeh. I am not one to fall in love
with a place so easily, but somehow, I cannot help

smiling at these palms, this foliage, these people,
or this wind that takes me way back home where

these shrubberies also grow wild in Monrovia.
I wonder what was on God's mind, San Diego, when

he made you? This sort of place makes my soul cry
for that other shoreline so far away, where home sits

by the sea, waiting, too, where the ocean is wild and hot.

II

RUINED CITY

I will bring back my exiled people ...
they will rebuild the ruined cities and live in them....

Amos 9: 15

Remembering Sodom

On the morning Sodom is to be burnt up,
Abraham tells Cousin Lot to warn his dear wife
not to go shopping or to the hair salon; not to use
any makeup or bring along heavy jewelry.

Then comes Mrs. Lot, after wasting the entire
morning on her hair and toenails, and her face
now glitters. On every finger, diamond rings
sparkle in the sun. Her eyes are so dark around

the lids, she can barely see anything without a touch
of mascara or dots of black in the picture. Why
would anyone wear these shoes on a day like this,
Lot wonders as the two lucky ones evacuate

the damned city. "Would God set everything on fire?"
Mrs. Lot asks the old man. "How lucky we are!"
Lot declares, even though Mrs. Lot is so angry,
she wants to die. Leaving all that gold and diamond

behind, all her banquet dresses and shoes. Leaving
her slave girls, and he says they're lucky? And her
sister, standing there like a carved stone? Unbelieving.
What about her mother, still in black, after her

father's death? Disbelief—the irony of a God burning
up a whole city. Would God burn this city with an old
woman still in black? What kind of daughter would
run away like this? And then she remembers a pair

of gold earrings, the ones with the fresh-cut diamonds
in the center, so heavy her earlobes burned each
time she'd worn them. They lay on the oak dresser,
next to her little gold statuette a friend had sent her.

In the Ruined City: A Poem for Monrovia

In the Ruined City, the water flaps lightly
against the beach at night.
It is August, after too many years,
the rain still pours down like stones.
The Atlantic always knows when to go to sleep,
but all the girls roam dark nights
and men have forgotten they are still men.

Monrovia has lost its name.

The ocean roars like wild fire.
It roars like a hungry lion at dawn,
like the whirlwind.
In the ruined city, all the girls
have legs made from plastic weapons,
and the boys pretend it is okay
for the once beautiful girls to walk
around on plastic legs.
There is little time for weeping,

and all the world stands silent.

There are no more trumpets or drums.
The Dorklor dancer who lost his legs
in the war now sits by the roadside, waiting.
It is something to lose your legs to a war,
they say, to Charles Taylor's ugly war,
where the fighter cannot recall why he still fights.

The men have forgotten they used to be men,
and the women sit by the roadside wondering
what has happened to this land.
If those outside of here do not come,
Liberia will drown in this rain.
Outside my window, the rain taps hard
in Old Road Sinkor, for my homecoming.

Only the rain knows how to cry.

Searching for Margaret

At the edge of the sea, the waves come and go.
It is a constant flapping all night.
There are no crowds and the ship is underwater
already. Only foamy waves flattened by time
remain, and the rust and oil that may have
been a part of the engine's doing.
Thoreau has been walking the beach all night,
by himself, barefoot. Every toe
has drunk its own share of all the water
meant for a toe.

It is a picture to see Thoreau's helpless
eyes; his hands do not understand
the sea waves or the sound of flapping water
or the foamy remains after a ship has gone down.
Margaret, if you had got lost in the woods,
where the green, green trees
keep the sun's hot glare from burning up
the woods, Thoreau would know the words
to say to bring you back. Thoreau,
who knows the sound of every cricket's squeaking,
the deep, low howling of wolves,
who knows how to keep the city at bay.
Margaret, it is a sad thing.

Today, I stopped by the beach where not just
the ship was wrecked, and there he was, flat, his old
rugged dark pants, soiled.
He'd been here an entire week, searching.
Waves aren't all that merciful to hand over
Margaret Fuller after giving up her child.
Or hand over the stories she'd been working on
all these years. Waves don't make great choices
you see—whether to let the dead couple
have their privacy—

But day after day, year after year, I go back
to see if the beach had given Thoreau back
to his woods. Today I sat at the edge of the
angry waves and wept with him.
Could I have I waited this many years
for a drowned friend?

City

At night, it is like fire
spreading beneath us.
This vast city
aflame, and the plane
groaning.

The city is more beautiful
from the sky at night.
At noon, it looks like
a worn-out garage,
a thing in the middle
of swamp country.

All the buildings are worn-out,
rusted to the bone
of steel, twisted
to make way so life
can go on.

Everything is bent and broken
along the hilltops.
I touch air to see if air
is still there.
The touchdown,

and we appear all worn-out,
too, like the city, broken.
All the birds
moved out long ago.
The trees too.

What the Land Carver Said from the Sky

From the sky I took this city and chopped it up into pieces.

This for you,
                    this for you,

this for you.

As for you, I give you the inner part,
where railroads slice up pieces of street and town.
Where the town crunches on its knees because
                    bullets have the right of way.

The train hoots, but I say the train cannot go by
on its tracks until the bullets pass.

And you who work so hard, pushing up into the jungle part—

after the factories arrived,
after the skyscrapers began to blossom on sharp needles
into sky, after parking lots clogged up air passages
in the ground—I ask you, ask you again,

why did you leave us here with your city?

After your men arrived with their bags of junk
that killed my brother and sent the others to jail.

And then you sent these bullets for reinvestment?

Why did you move away from the lot I carved up for you?

Until the Plane Drops

At two in the morning, I sit at the edge of my bed
because I want to see how the world will destroy itself.

That's why some people sleep with their dog in bed.
A dog will bark even at four a.m., that most solitary

hour of the morning. They say it was that same
hour during which all of Jesus' disciples fell asleep,

before the Roman guards arrived. A dog will yelp
or bark or howl before the atomic bomb falls, before

the blast goes off. A dog can see a falling bomb even
at midnight. Back in my home country, everyone

is fleeing home before *Taylor* and his men finally
destroy us all. But the people in my new town don't

know how the wars we can't see will consume us all
someday. We are hiding underneath our blankets,

and at work, we talk about the hot sun and the snow
and the trees coming out of hiding after winter.

We talk about vacations in the mountains and on
the beaches and the new software that will set

the pace in today's world. We love the things that
don't matter at all. My professor says to write poetry

about the surreal, about invisible goddesses in the sky,
the goddesses we'll never know. That's because it is

an abomination to know the world's pain. That's
because we're afraid that when the airline stewardess

tells us how to place the air mask over our faces before
the air goes out, when all that's left to us is empty

space, and the plane is about to crash, she really is
telling us to shut our eyes tight until the plane drops.

Retriever

Sometimes I see a railway
where cheating husbands
line up, waiting for a train that only hoots
and hoots for no one

because it was not meant to hoot
or blow or honk.
Every unfaithful man should stand
waiting for that train
that never comes or never stops
or never was, where the invisible
woman sits biting her nails
in expectation,

until the train itself
or the idea of the train becomes lost
and the woman is not there
anymore, and the train,
as if moving backwards erases
its own tracks because
it was not even there.

Come to think of it,
it was only the men waiting
there for the never-coming train.
It is only the men waiting
there forever, and you, there
waiting among those unfaithful
men without end.
But as I watch you not from the road,
but from my eyeglasses,

there was no one, no woman,
no men, only you,
and no eyeglasses with which
to see anything but the air.
And the air was not even
there for you to breathe.
And then I decided to retrieve
you from this world
forever.

All Dirges Have Ceased

All dirges shall cease at the striking of the clock,
at seven, when dusk comes creeping with death.
No more dirges will be sung for those taken away
or slaughtered or cramped together in camps
around the world—this our war.
Until we all wither like charred remains
of brush after the wild fire burns itself out.
And all the living creatures that once owned
the forest lie about in dry ash.

A snail shell, half burnt, a rattlesnake, coiled,
after the fire has eaten away its flesh.
A scorpion and her entire family, as if smoked
or parched hard for the ground.
And animals that used to run wild
in the jungles are all dead. But who will dare
mourn the passing of mere animals when
humans are still perishing and being smoked
and buried alive and put on the line

for the executioner, who is our warlord?
Where is everyone as Kwashiorkor saps away
our war children one by one?
Our warlord tells us we cannot wail or mourn
or sing a dirge and wear black lappas or bury
the dead or send a letter abroad to tell those
who do not know about our dead.

Today when the sun comes into the kitchen
through the kitchen door or window, let us
catch its shadow, its rays; let us lock up the sun
in a box, in a steel box and put a padlock
on the box. So tomorrow, there will be no sunlight
for the whole world. Tomorrow.
So there will be no more sunlight tomorrow.

An Elegy for the St. Peter's Church Massacred

I fled the war in that first ceasefire.
Missing all the other wars, the other massacres,
the burning and re-burning of Monrovia,

the silencing again of those who had already
been silenced in that first sweep.
My neighbors envied me through dark-eyed lashes,
skeletal cheekbones and hunger.

I envy those who were massacred.
Those who never saw their killers approach
with heavy bootsteps that made no sound
in the dark morning hours.

Those who died in colonies, in one huge group
at the *President's* order.
They arrived in death, holding hands—
mothers, hugging their babies, men,
helping their wives over the hills of death;
talking, laughing, singing,
they walked happily in death.

It is such a good thing to go with company.

The Atlantic's wailing winds at the hurried steps
of hundreds of soldier boots
will live forever with the living.

I honor those who were massacred
at St. Peter's Lutheran by troops
with only an errand to run.
The raining of guns upon sleeping people
as if this were not already July.

How I envy those who never heard those
stalking bootsteps at the church doors that night;
never saw the faces of their murderers,
never had to count the hours remaining—
only one shot, and it was all over.

When we wept with Glayee, who arrived
clinging to two toddler girls at Soul Clinic
Refugee camp, how could I envy her?
Haunted eyes, scarred arms and legs from
climbing up that barbed wire fence, a slashed wrist
from where they spilled her own blood
in sacrificial offering.

It is a sad story when we survive the massacre
of hundreds who were only sleeping before God.
It is a sad story when one survives
the massacre of the whole world like that.

The Morning After: An Elegy

My husband and I gather our remaining lives
the morning after. I snatch away memories
of childhood, adolescence, college, where my life

was a bittersweet of books, boys, my father's
discipline, politics, and the whole world spread
out, awaiting me. This morning's bombing

is again rocking our lives and our home. A single
suitcase will have to bear all this pain.
It is August 1, 1990, right after a number no

one could count were massacred in deep sleep;
today, taken before today. They lay all over
St. Peter's Lutheran, in the aisles, on the solid

wood pulpit, twisted, in classrooms on top of one
another, a child here, a mother there, a father here,
a baby there, a heap here, a few there, our tattered

history. Where was God at two o'clock in the morning?
How did those soldiers push aside church doors,
reason, God? And is there anyone who can tell

my wide-eyed children how a single order could
put hundreds to death? To explain how hundreds
of troops could empty hundreds of bullets while

the world sits by? So we pack boxes of books, pots,
suitcases of clothes, stereos; we fold mattresses
and chairs, shutting blinds, windows, turning

off waterless taps so if water ever returns while
we're gone, this home will not become a river.
These new circumstances of our lives now gather

mucus in my throat. All this time, our three starving
dogs are watching; no barking, no jumping, are they
also wondering if someone will explain where

we're going? One last wave for my watchdogs before
refugee camps, starvation, then flight for America.
But everyone couldn't come to America, you see.

Ceasefire Christmas—1990

Again, it is Christmas, and in the market places
Christmas is everywhere...
fine, fine dresses, Fanti lappa suits,
batik gowns and bubbas, cheap coat suits
and flamingo skirts, tailored by the hands
of Mandingos and Fulani in town.

Monrovia tailors will weave gold and silver
threads into tie-dye and batik pieces
so passerby shoppers will buy—
Today, money will pass from hand to hand...
so much money coming and going through
rough hands, big, stiff hands, soft, rich hands,
Big Mammie hands.
                            Waterside Mammies will carry
heavy money bags under big, fat bellies.
All that money tied up under
dangling belly buttons—
No one needs to tell you Christmas is here.

Yanna Boys, up and down, dragging heavy,
aluminum pots, balloons and plastic dolls,
slippers and what have you.
Big Mammies, their big, wide *tumbas* and long
bargaining hands, calling us to buy lappas,
to buy their almost fresh palm oil and fish.

                            That was before the wars...
Christmas could not come without the slaughter
of roosters and goats, without the slaughter of sheep,
of fatty pigs and cows,
without some Bassa woman leaving her man
because he didn't buy that lappa
and that matching pair of shoes;
without some Monrovia woman packing up

because she didn't get that new icebox
or that new car; without some village woman
running to Monrovia
to find her own Monrovia Christmas man.

In Monrovia, they say men come so cheap,
you can get a man at street corners.
Monrovia with its blinking lights and honking cars.
                    That was before the war...
Christmas could not come without neighbors
at my door on Christmas Eve, wanting fish,
meat, rice so their children could also eat;
without neighbor children
crowding my doorway on Christmas afternoon
for more jollof rice and baked chicken.
African beat, rocking in the Christmas fever.

A drunkard, down the road,
                    running out of four-letter words.

It is Christmas, 1990, so I wait at my doorway
for neighbors to come for fish and pork meat or rice,
cake and sweets even though I now starve.
I wait for Christmas children, dressed
in loud colors and ribbons. I wait for neighbors
who didn't make it back alive in this Cease-fire.

            In the yard, bushes grow wild over the dead.

Christmas doves are gathering for their ritual
in my backyard. It is Christmas,
but no cars coming, no family talking loud,
no street carolers, no Santa Claus and his troupe
to dance up dust for a quarter, a dime
or some dollar notes that won't buy a fish.

On the radio, they say it is Cease-fire now,

my people, they say it is cease fire,
so I stand at my doorway, waiting
for the ocean wind to pass over the silent brush,
over my roof, over the Harmattan.

I wait for the ocean wind to pass....

For Kwame Nkrumah

When the news came that you had died, your sons
gathered in the front way, and did not know why

they gathered. Smoke in the fireplace curled upwards,
and the elders said how good it was that you'd left

so much smoke behind. When dawn comes, we need
the ash, we need the charred wood and chips of wood

to light the new fire. Every day needs its own fire since
no one borrows one night's moonlight for another night.

Kwame, Osagyefo, sharp eyes that saw the history we
now live. When you died, there we were. We gathered

to hear the sad news, and told our mute selves how strong
you had left us even though we knew how truly weak

we had become. Today we've burnt up all the shrines
you built, shrines of times to come; the vision we saw

in your eyes has perished with time. We cannot even find
our way back to where you stood, proclaiming that someday-—

Africa would be free, one day, Africa would be truly one,
you said. Today, I saw our ancestral masks on sale here

in America, downtown Kalamazoo at the Black Arts Festival.
The very shrines, now doomed artifacts, something you

never told us about. That they would burn down everything
we had? That they would bring our own relics to stand

between us and the new world, just in case someone needs
to cover their immaculate walls? That we would buy

our own treasures from corner streets downtown America?
Your photo was downtown Kalamazoo too, on sale,

blown up by the artist who blows up other people's ancestors
for sale. They have brought back our masks, masks from

years and years ago, Kwame. A woman next to me fiddled
with the mask, turning it side to side. You could still see

the white chalk, white mud from ages of living in the shrines.
Other peoples' gods, other peoples' ancestral relics in

other peoples' land. If you could come and see the castles
you built, or see the sons you carved up the land for, Kwame,

who knows if you would laugh or cry or sigh or just stand
there while the rain pours down your face. Kwame, they

are making new books about you now. Your enemies
know how to tell your story better than your friends.

If the World Ceases to Be Now

When the stars stop short, the light
in the distance turns yellow.
Leaves turn cold, snap and fall,
and there is no need for grass or grasshopper
and the firefly loses its thrifty light.
And then the river rushes for salt to the ocean,
ceasing its rushing, caked salt
waiting on a sandy beach; all is lost on
the snail shell and water pebbles
and on the old sand.
If the world ceases to be now, I will
understand. The pearl, waiting in
the clam's hard shell stops short
and melts with the tide.
There are no water lilies, and from now on,
there will be no sunshine until my mother
takes her place where no raindrops
may interrupt her good day.

Something Death Cannot Know

My husband and I stole away from the camp one day
to see if it was now safe to come back home, from the war.

We pushed open the double oak doors, and in our living
room, a few pots laid here and there; no water,
no lights, no clothing—everything gone.

Outside, you could count the deep rocket holes.
Splinters from fallen rockets could fill buckets
after months of bombing.

I stood in the middle of what used to be my hallway, my
house, my world, counting holes in the walls;
the house now leaked. Windows, partly blown out.

On the floor, my Sunday dresses lay trashed about, where
looters had dropped them in that sudden rush.
I watched the sun come in, through cracked glass

of windows, through the holes in the walls, where
only missile splinters could have passed—
But I was home again.

When I saw the birds, they chirped and began to fly
from overgrown brushes. Then the wind blew
in from the river, cold November winds from the river.

The Atlantic's moist winds from the other side over
the hills from the beach, where the ocean's restless waves
howl away days.

The scent of sweet blossoms, oregano mix,
and mint in the air. Flowers in what used to be my yard,
wild. I sat on the floor,

on the cold ceramic tiles of what used to be my living room
and laughed loud, hard, until my husband rushed inside
to see if I was still okay.

I laughed until I began to weep. Glad to be alive, to be here,
to know a town that had become ghost, to get acquainted
with the birds and the flowers and the river

and the winds for the first time. To know life
in its subtle creeping—when only crickets matter.

To know that after all this, my children were still alive,
that Mama was alive still, and life remembered
I used to live here.

The sun touching my now flabby arms told me I was here.
After all that bombing, here was I.
To know that there is something death cannot know—

Under the Rubble

The day arrived through broken steel
and glass, amidst the sunshine,
this already broken world,
becoming shreds.

Ever since that day,
I have been trying to see how anyone
can crash a plane into a tower,
planes filled with so many
into two towers.
A jetliner that has learned how to defy

gravity, obeying orders—lost orders
from lost people.
Its hot metal body emitting steam and fuel,
all its seats that were arranged
so life is preserved during flight

in every kind of turbulence.
My brain cells weep each time my memory
re-seats me on those planes, in a row next
to those four hijackers.
They are biting oily nails and lips, biting

their tongues, gulping down
thick mucus of tears because all this time,
they know how they will massacre
an entire generation of us,
a whole world of us.

No one can plot this kind of tragedy
without their whole body breaking loose
in anger against them.
Will they ever know the extent to which
they have lost their own war?

My head spins now as the jetliner
begins that swerve, that turn into
the World Trade Center, so all of us
can become just ashes.
Over and over, I find myself seated

on those planes, again and again,
in tears, my eyes shut tight. Sometimes,
I'm seated at the cockpit door,
wide-eyed, as the men rush past me
for the cockpit. I cannot get myself
off the planes

as we crash again and again into the building,
and my chest explodes again and again.
I am that number, those who were not counted,
could never have been.
I am afraid of being numbered,
the abstractness

of Roman numerals after a tragedy.
The fear of being counted, of being numbered,
the crooked twist of numbers.
There is always someone else, I tell myself,
after the three thousand,
there is always someone else
under the rubble.

III

UMBILICAL CORDS

A mother is a mother still,
The holiest thing alive.

—Samuel Taylor Coleridge

Coming Home: For Besie-Nyesuah

Besie runs towards me, arms wide, despite the crowd
at the airport, she's screaming, "Mo-mm-m-m-ie,"

and everybody stares. Arms around me, my daughter
holds me tight, and we almost fall beside her suitcase

I have just lifted off the belt. At nineteen, she is now
a woman, tall, slender, her soft, small arms and fair skin

remind me of Ma Wadeh, my mother-in-law. In a moment,
I am looking her all over, counting to see if she is not

too skinny for a girl her age. Every girl becomes woman
when she can come home, knowing how like her mother

she is becoming—a woman like all the other women
before her. "This is Pittsburgh," I say, "Isn't it beautiful?"

We're driving past houses in the distant hills along
Pittsburgh's winding freeway, houses that lean and rush

past us as we also rush past them. Everything here leans
sideways, almost free, as if to fall into the merging rivers

down below. My college-age children are coming home
to Pennsylvania, where we are surrounded by hills

and valleys and cliffs, and the university where my
new students speak with an accent they refuse to admit.

"So this is home now?" Besie says as if to herself
while I turn into our new driveway in a neighborhood

of rolling hills and brick houses overlooking one another.
"We are the first black on this property," I say. But this

is going to be home—all these valleys and green, green hills
will be home. "But this is Pennsylvania," Besie says, as doors

bang and everyone rushes out to welcome her home after
too many months away. "We are all trying to find home,"

I say, as my words become lost in the din of screaming
children and my husband, lifting Besie up in the air

and swinging her around in circles. All my children
are under one roof again, I tell myself, for the first

time, all my children are under one roof in our new state.
But Michigan is that ghost that stands at the outskirts

of your new town, where your memory refuses to shut out
so many years, and that year when you arrived with

nothing and looking to find home among strangers,
where the cold, cold winds became a new friend.

Your second chance at finding home, now becoming
memory too. Michigan haunts the holidays, another

ghost to carry around among all the other ghosts we are
seeking to undo. In Monrovia, families will gather

and discuss the many years we have been away from
home. Monrovia is the true ghost story of lost peoples

in the Diaspora. In America, we are the new nomads,
the wanderers coming home or looking to make

home or running away from home among new people,
and, one by one, our children, who will never know

where we really come from, are leaving only to come
back to decorative lights, Christmas trees, holiday

music, and turkey baking in the oven, stuffing,
and pies. We are becoming new people, I tell myself.

When My Daughter Tells Me She Has a Boyfriend

When my daughter tells me she has a boyfriend now,
at college, where we send our children so they can
grow up some more, I ask her, "Is he black...or...
white...?" There is just silence, no phone clicking,
no whisper. No pauses are allowed between a mother
and her daughter who has gone to college
to find herself among many lost people.

"What sort of question is that?" she sighs.
The phone has learned how to talk back
in many ways. "Is he tall or short? Are his eyes
large and round and brown like the walnut
just before it becomes meal? Are they green-green
or are they blue, pale, after the color of sky
just before gray settles in upon them in September?"
"Mom..." my daughter is weeping now.
My daughter has learned to weep at last
about the things that really matter.

"Are you racist?" My daughter cries into the phone.
Only a phone knows how to ask such questions.
It is only a far-away phone, a far-away daughter
taking liberty with phones, asking
a perfect mother if she is racist.

"Racism is something that happens to me," I say.
Doesn't a mother have the right to know,
to know it all, to have it all plain and simple on the table,
all the things one needs to know?
Whether my daughter is bringing home a tall
black boy, so dark, his skin sparkles,
a boy with hair he spends many nights
grooming so it loses all its nappy?

But my daughter tells me she's going home
with her boyfriend—home to his mother,
another woman, a white woman who will

stand at her doorstep hugging
my first girl-child, the daughter of a bull,
Jabbeh *Cho, Koo-oo-koo-oo,* an off-shoot
of Nganlun, where the spring water bubbles
at noonday in March. My daughter from
Seo Paton, the woman from Wah, losing her way
in a land where we are all trying to find ourselves.

My daughter, the women from Seo are hot like pepper.
They do not run off to meet their boyfriend's mother
just like that, girl. But in America,
a girl can hop on a car or plane, on a truck, or whatever
to meet her boyfriend's family at eighteen,
before her mother has looked the boy over,

before the elders sit in upon the whole idea
of a boyfriend, to see if it's taboo to marry a boy
from another clan. "What are his people like?
Who is his father? Does his father come from
a great people, a great clan?" I wanted to ask.

In America, a child at eighteen can drive a car,
run over a deer at two o'clock in the morning,
gather their belongings at noon, and move
out, at sixteen. I have heard it all.

My girl child whose beauty shines like the moon,
over the hilltops, over the forest when
the sun comes out in December, in Tugbakeh.
Nyeneplu, the beautiful, my daughter
running off to meet the other woman,
my daughter who reminds me of Neferteri
on her throne. My daughter, a woman like myself.
When I see that boy, I will cook him spicy pepper soup
so he knows how the dodo cries at night
just before the hawk has time to flee.

Monrovia Revisited

This is the city that killed my mother.
Its crooked legs bent
from standing too long,
waiting so angry people can kill
themselves too.

No more grass along street corners—
so many potholes from years of war.
Immigrants from all over the globe
used to come here
on tender feet,

in search of themselves.
Abandoned city—
a place that learned
how to cry out loud even though
nobody heard.

This is the city where I first learned
how to lose myself.
Windy city, blue ocean city.
They say a city on a hill
cannot be hid.

The city of salty winds, salty tears,
where stubborn people still hold
us hostage after Charles Taylor.
You should come here if you want
to know how sacred
pain can be.

August 11, 2003

I sit at the edge of my bed where the bedroom
is another place in which one may go into oneself.

Charles Taylor and his family are boarding
a plane in Monrovia.
On TV, Charles Taylor is climbing
on to a jetliner,
leaving.

Someone has decided he should leave on a plane,
not by drowning or by a bullet, not by
an explosion or by execution.

Someone has given him a beautiful place
where he can sit and smoke
and toast a drink to the hundreds of thousands
he has already killed.

The phone beside my bed is ringing.

All over the world, phones are ringing
themselves mute in solemn duty—
All over the world,
phones are ringing today.

But the words of my heart have become
lost thoughts. Fourteen years,
and I'm like a dead woman.

My heart has a big hole where all the
stories no one has heard, linger forever.
Where stories become scarred,

where there is no solace
for the grieved and the dead.

When my father finally comes through,
the phone seems dead—only the muffles
of his weary voice.

After fourteen years, my father has also
lost his voice to describe the years.

Untitled Pieces at the Corner Bar

We have given him too many hours to hold.
His minutes scattered around him like new fruit flies.

A few minutes to spread out on the city streets
where boys and girls stand puffing at air

and who knows what else they puff? Too many
days to hold in between a child's bare hands.

His mother lingers late at work, then bars, where
she sits chattering the night away as if on a plate—

her beer bubbles and foams and moans. "Other
people will rise tomorrow from their beds

and find new solitudes away at lakes," she tells
the other woman at the corner bar downtown.

My friends have brought me here to celebrate
another friend who is retiring at a lake near us.

The woman stares at me and begins to tell her story
about the boy left at home. "You cannot argue

with money," she tells the other woman. Tomorrow
at the lake we will find luxuries where one cannot

argue with the luxury of winds and boats and BBQs
and the water's cold touch on wrinkling skin.

I am that woman, sitting in her body, and I carry
her little boy whose entire life story she tells over

and over during the hour. "One day," she tells my ear
even though her words are actually for the other

woman's ears, "I will walk away from those children
and never come back," she sighs, "one day,

I will walk away and never come back to this world."

In a Moment When the World Stops

One solemn moment, a star falls
through sky like fireflies.
What was it you said when the bomb exploded
in Oklahoma, and in a moment, hundreds who did not
call in sick for work that day lay among rubble?
In between stubborn walls and steel,
walls becoming plain dirt?

The day my husband told me to give the rest
of my life in all of its bareness of plain laughter,
to go to bed on the same bed beside him and bear
our children and be his friend forever, I smiled,
not knowing. In the restaurant, I stared at the walls
to see if anything would move.
Did anything dare to move that day?

When the plane is in mid-sky and over the Atlantic,
or when pilot and crew have no clue where it is,
passengers resting at dawn,
a watch somewhere ticks and moves with the plane,
and then suddenly, a voice announces how
in a moment this plane will be gone,
the voice summing up every
living breath on the plane the way

a mathematician adds figures on a bare sheet.
That everyone should prepare for the crash,
prepare to go down somewhere into uncharted
territory. That moment of eye meeting soul,
between passengers and crew,
the clock's minute hand takes the moment
away, and the moment refuses to be explained.

How a baby's miniature hand may rest upon
a mother's, white sheets, white walls, white
everything, the infant's eyes, so unsure
of the world, and the world standing still too?

Today, like a child, I stand beside my husband
as always, in the hospital room as he lies still,
in preparation for the landing.
A parachute can bear the weight of a man
at the onset of midlife.

They will cut his skin aside, dark skin, then red, fat
and all, peeled away by white hands.
The doctor will again prove how we are all alike inside.
Eye, meeting eye, my husband grins,
words slipping into thin air, where words
can let a woman down. I will be here
when you wake up, I say,
I will be here when you wake up, I say.

After the Memorial

Today, another student died at school. Another boy
at twenty, another sophomore, another woman's only son.

A girl in my class told me the news just before my ten
o'clock class. She said, it was his heart—a bad heart.

Something that was always a part of him, she said.
Something in his heart was always loose—a thin line

somewhere. Where the heart was supposed to tighten
to pump blood from the heart to the brain to the hands

to the feet and belly buttons to the toes and back again
to the heart. Something must have snapped, she said.

Stephanie, a girl almost looking nineteen or twenty
or twenty-one or something. Bloody eyes, red hair, she

stood at my desk in tears, there she stood. Was I the priest
or counselor or something? The delicate lines already

making their way under her eyelids. This was her friend,
her boyfriend, her best friend. He was tall and blond

and smart and funny and walked like he'd bought the campus
and the whole world with just his looks. Someone told me

afterwards, it was heroin overdose and alcohol overdose
and everything overdose. No one called the police.

In a college dorm, where the party can run over the rim
of every glass and the fumes from everything everywhere

in the party room can penetrate every fabric of everything
alive, and everyone is red-eyed because something

else is smelling. And you know it is often too late to call
the police or the ambulance, and, of course, not his parents.

He was supposed to come to, they'd said, on the floor where
everybody left him so he could come to. Last year, another

student died—my student—at home, in a bed that belonged
to him, where the sheets and the mattress were soft

and white and cool and personal. The sheets understood
the matter more plainly. They belonged to him. It was drug

overdose, someone said. When the news came on the phone,
I was at home. Tuesday—not a day for news. The Dean from

campus called to break the news to me. Why me, I thought.
I was scared. His Mom had asked to break the news gently

to this one teacher. She will take it hard, and my son loved
her like family, she'd said. I rushed to my bathroom, my

stomach boiling when I heard. All the hours I'd spent
tutoring this one kid until his writing skills, which had nothing

to do with his writing skills, sharpened. His words had taken
on color and detail and precision just so he would die?

He had died quietly in his sleep, I was told. At the college
dinner after the memorial, his Mom held my hand tight,

staring. "He was our only child, you know." Silence.
"I understand completely," I said. "I understand incompletely."

Leaving: A Poem for Gee

Today, Gee shows me what it means to pick up and leave.
Boxes on top of boxes, where a shoelace refuses to stay

in a teenager's moving-away storage. "Mom," he says,
"the next time we move away to a new town, find

a new church for singing and clapping and youth groups,
where everyone cares where you're going when you

have to leave. Talk to someone please, Mom, talk to
someone who knows someone in the new church, in

that new town, and in that neighborhood so there is
someone to speak to when I arrive, and when I have

to leave, so there will be someone I can leave behind."
Sometimes, night can be like that you see, the invisible

act, the disappearing people we are, when like dark
shadows or the moon and the fireflies, suddenly, we are

no longer there, and yet no one wonders. In another few
days, we will be gone from this small town of unfamiliar

people who never knew we were even passing through
like this. In Byron Center, where we used to live—that

small Michigan Dutch town of small houses, a church
here, a church there, kind people with old stories of having

arrived on ships in the World War. A town where no one
ever went anywhere because now, they all belonged.

My next door neighbor's father used to own his house
before him, after his great-grandfather died, leaving

him the house. Small town, small secrets, huge memories,
where the ground is hardened not by anger alone. I am

that other stranger seeking to find roots and ground
and a place where even the squirrel can run free, where

the squirrel also belongs to me. War is such a mystery,
such an unexplained phenomenon, an unexplained

grassland, the indefensible stories of seekers. But no one
clings to those seeking for that new homeland, where

memory can find place again. Outside my house, people
refuse to take on to the newcomer or see or ask questions.

They made their friends long ago while I was still in
the Liberian war or before I was even born. So when

I move away tomorrow, I will leave behind only a house
on a bare street corner, where flowers bloom not just

in the spring, a place where the cherry tree at my
front yard blooms pink petals every spring and sheds

them thoughtlessly in the rain, and the green lawn across
the road sits quietly, and the neighbors, mute as death.

The Golden Retriever barks all night long, as the cricket
loses track of its own singing. Big mounds of iron hills

rolling, and the neighbor woman's child presses her nose
against the window glass, my invisible neighbor.

I am leaving behind no one at all, don't get me wrong;
this is the new life where only the ghost lives. I am the

blessed one with just one small daughter and a son, a
husband, another son, and another daughter, taken

by the wind. Someone once asked me why people like us
move around so much; why can't we balance feet between

the hills and the sloping crevasses of this new life, between
these old cliffs and the valleys, and I say, "I do not know."

While I Wait for the War

I used to say, "When the war ends, we will go back home."
To the sea and the river, where the humid sun turns miles
of marshland behind my house into solid ground.
At night, the moon lends light to my chicken coop.

Back home, where it's okay when your Auntie you've
never ever seen comes in, speaking impeccable Grebo,
talking of how she carried you on her back when you
were just this tall, cleaned your pupu bottom,

ate the snot from your nose when you had the cold, then
whipped your butt because you couldn't stop using
those four-letter words. Now she comes wanting money
to zinc her roof, a house she was building before
your Ma first met your Pa.

Home, where the home is a mansion, but the road that leads
there winds up and down forgotten, rocky hills no car can climb.
Where the President's mistress is your college classmate,
but it's okay, because he's President, you know.

At home if you're not careful, you can find your own head
right on your doorstep in the morning, before the rooster
crows, your head left there by the President's men,
but it's still okay. Where Bai was your Grandfather,

boasting of all the warriors who fought to give him this land
he thought he owned until he was dead and gone.
Now come some rebels with guns....
So, I sit on the carpet here in America, the way
a Grebo woman sits on The Mat,

my legs stretched out, and I holler, crying because today
the phone told me that Ma had died at home, two weeks ago,
and I didn't even know. I get up after one long hour of crying,
go to the window and cry some more.

On the streets in Byron Center, cars still speed, people
still mow their lawns, water their fresh, green grass
just to mow again tomorrow. My neighbors wash,
then wax their cars; wash, then wax their cars.
Today, you know, Ma Nmano's news came in, dead,

my mother dead, and I'm here waiting for the war
at the window, my blouse wet. I cry loud, then low, when
news comes in that Nyanken Hne is dead, and Sunny, too,
dead, everyone, dead. I cry one dirge after the other,
for Uncle Henry Toe who died just after the cease-fire,

couldn't wait to see Taylor crowned president. Cry for T.K.,
executed for being a policeman, for Ma Nandi,
my mother-in-law in the Ivory Coast, who refused to die
on foreign ground. For Borbor Kweesay, Sehseh Kimah...

and after eight years, I'm still crying dirges.
So I buy a house, a car, to look like I'm settling, to replace
what the war took away. I write a book for everyone
to read the stories.... Sometimes I want to just get up
and walk back home.

Where the dodo still wakes us in Tugbakeh and the hawk
enters the chicken coop on a farm far away at Gbaliah-De,
and we children run because the roosters are ready for battle
with the hawk for snatching away one of theirs.
In the market, you can buy fish between clattering voices,

returning home with the morning news, fresh
from the lips of market women. I've come back to school
to read more books...to write about my children turning
into foreigners right under my roof.
They eat beef, roasted in spicy-hot pepper.

I stew them cassava leaves, palaver sauce cooked in red palm
oil from Ghana, gari from Nigeria. My house smells of Africa,
Asia, and America while my children grow like coconut trees.
They eat palm butter on steamed rice, okra stewed with
smoked fish, pig's feet and shrimp—

then eat ice cream on Dutch apple pie. My children swallow
fufu in spicy pepper soup, then stand there,
rocking to American Hip-Hop, while I wait for the war.
In the meantime, they will grow up without the Dorklor,

without the pounding of dozens of drums, where the dancer
always knows which beat to dance to. While Gborbelloh
throws us under great illusions, dancers blow dust about.
Without Iyeeh's spider tales, weaving a hundred webs
from which any of us may dangle free.

IV

WOMAN

She shall be called Woman.

—*Genesis 2:23*

In the Making of a Woman

In the making of a woman,
the navel string is cut, ears pierced,
and the beads firmly tied
around her waist, neck, ankles.
Iyeeh does not give in to the infant's loud screaming.
After all, she must be made a woman
in every sense that a Grebo woman can be.

Then the naming ritual must begin.
The recounting of histories
she may never hear repeated
except the day she brings forth
another like herself.
Nothing must go wrong here,
not even a sneeze.
The ceremony, with perfection
if she must be a woman.

And then, though with beads strung
all over her, Iyeeh calls
in the elders, and the libation begins.
Chanting so solemnly, the baby in her
quits screaming, and she is let
upon the world—a Grebo woman
is let loose upon our innocent world.

Taboo

Arrangements for my coming
into the world
are incomplete pieces

of letters and promises,
a clause that ends with a cough,
a deep sigh

in the middle of a sentence,
that one sentence
that was not said—

the knowing and not knowing
how other girls left
their babies

in buckets and outdoor toilets,
went to school the next day
with well-ironed

skirts, combed hair, and a smile.
I was the word you didn't say—

strong-willed fetus,
refusing

to go away, the half dried
lappa on the clothesline
in April.

And Mama,
the dropout,
just so I could be
me.

A Winding Trail

My mother carried me upside down, pushed me out
     like a crab, sideways.

The children in our town could not place my name in line
     with other names. All those Iyeeh

who could not sing my praise names right, mumbled
     each time I passed. My naming ritual stood still

so thunder would roll. Libation waiting, the kola nuts
slowly bleeding the bowl of water red. Out of nowhere,

a mucus-face child sneezed, and Iyeeh mumbled about
the kinds of spices, the mix of peppers she'd ground

     into the ceremonial blend of pungent,
eye-watering pepper; how long she'd rubbed the lump

     upon the pepper rock; hot pepper seeds
crushed by Iyeeh's old hands.

     God, you know how an old woman
will carry on about a thing like that?

The clansman from my father's town arrived; feet dusty,
     sweat, streaming down his dark face even though

it was just dawn. The calabash of libation fell and broke,
     and Bai forgot what my name was to be.

"Lahwloh," Bai shook his head.
     Lahwloh—to calm my mother's heart,

"Be patient in this life." The elders bowed their heads—
         Absolute consent.
The Oracles agreed, and I becoming, Lahwloh-Jlajeh.

Libation—chanting,
libation—chanting.

So may it be, in unison, the elders and the oracles,

and then I screamed when someone slapped my bottom.
                    This was a lack of reverence
coming from a newborn, someone said. Iyeeh bowed

and chuckled at a stone on the rocky ground—
I would make a tough wife someday, Iyeeh said.

All these years, Iyeeh tells this story still, in winding trails.
One day, it was the washing water that was spilled,

a boy's, not a girl's sneeze. It was lightning that caused
                    the spill, not the clansman or the sneeze.
My life has been a winding trail.

You want to know my past, don't you, God?

I grew up, spreading legs and arms in all directions,
like the paw-paw tree behind Iyeeh's hut.

"A coconut tree never grows flesh if it must grow so tall,"
        Iyeeh says. And then I met my father—light-light

skinned like the inside of a pumpkin. His hair looking
                    as if it had been washed in palm oil,
dabbled over the fire for a shine, flattened to his scalp.

Where was he while I grew?
                    Lahwloh, a lone stump,
all my roots clipped so other trees would grow.

Stories

Someone will tell my story when I'm gone.
Someone will come into my house and look
at all these boxes on top of each other,
and all these papers I have wanted
to write something on.
The stories I carry around like a pregnant woman
who cannot say when she got pregnant—
They will be spilled all over
in invisible tidbits. People will say how
she was this and how she was that,

but no one will know all the stories I carry around
like a garbage truck.
The stories that coil like an earthworm
after the rain. The sight of an earthworm—
something not only children will scream at.
Maybe someone will write them for me—
The stories about my brother, Toh,
crashing my father's yellow taxi
with my father seated right there beside him.

The taxi wanting to protect Toh from
my father's anger—the taxi that was meant
to set Toh on that career track at last.
Pa, always wanting to turn little people's
dreams into his own. Carving our lives
as though we were some pieces of wood
or wood dust on his carving table.
And the other stories, the ones about
me beating up that boy just because
he called me *Marie Biscuit.*

All the other neighborhood children
standing there while we still lived on the Bye Pass.
Me, beating up a boy, and Pa,
laughing and clapping when he heard

how his daughter had gone and beat up a strong boy.
One woman that will beat up the boys,
Pa said, laughing and walking to his room,
looking like a small child coming home
with his first prize trophy. But yet, there
are the other stories nobody will ever know.

Ruined Trails

We used to walk these trails along Bai's farmstead
at Gbaliah-De. Its razor bushes extending sharp blades
and thorny brambles in rough welcome.

As though we were children, forever and aimless.
At the old farmstead, Iyeeh's hut humped wearily
beneath the hill, waiting, even though the years

and the rain had eaten away soil beneath its legs.
And Iyeeh, sitting here at her doorpost as if for years
she'd kept her eyes upon the narrow, dusty

village street, pleading for our return. Iyeeh isn't
here anymore, like Gbaliah-De, she's gone.
Was Gbaliah-De burnt down...bombed?

Did it give in to the rocking when missiles broke
loose upon village, city and town?
The giant rubber trees still stand, defying,

where coffee and cocoa have lost their way.
And the pumpkin has wound its way through these
ruined trails, spreading orange flowers along the road.

Stranger Woman

In the village, the old women pull her out,
the afterbirth and all. She is dashed into

wrinkled, welcoming hands, then a warm lappa
embraces her as the old women chant praise names

from here to faraway places, and then the blessings.
Iyeeh ties up, then snaps off the navel string, then

washes the newborn woman who is screaming
throat, tongue, and guts out. Then the beading

begins—wrists, ankles, neck, waist, all stringed
up. This new woman, who is now bound.

After that, the piercing of soft ears so earrings will
pass through. Little black threads strung in place

until the earrings arrive. Then the naming is done,
and maybe there'll be a Rooster's Feather

stuck in her dark, curly hair, and she's betrothed
to some man, who himself is only a child.

He may never discover how she was destined
to re-create or destroy him someday. In the village,

you may find her walking to school, after discarding
those birthing beads for puberty, her breasts

sharp like needles, or maybe, on the farm road,
she walks, now married before the breasts

are even formed, practicing on the way to market,
dirges she will sing at the funeral of her father-in-law

whom she dislikes terribly. In the city, you may
find the stranger woman who is so many girls

at the same time; in college, or a high school
dropout; maybe, a single mother who takes home

the latest baby to her mother, or you may find her
in the doctor's office, beneath white jacket, the doctor.

The stranger woman, now a mother, a wife, or maybe
not even a wife or a mother, not a daughter, because

having left home, she's found no other fireplace
that will take in the son's wife as if she were

a daughter. Stranger woman, giving up mother,
father, sister, brother, all the smell of cooking

which having shaped her, has let her go. In a new
town with husband or in a new country, you may

find her on a road, following other people's dreams,
or maybe, not even following other people's dreams.

Mammie Wata

Those who see Mammie Wata are equipped
with eyes of steel, forever scarred

by the memory of her beauty, the memory
of Mammie Wata standing upon water waves—
that stare of hers.

When we saw her or when we thought
we saw her, there she stood,
in the middle of the Atlantic,

away from the beach where children
still go swimming today.
The sun so hot, even the ocean begins to sweat.

It was Friday, after school.
Children who do not listen to their mothers
run to the beaches along Monrovia's shores.

Some of them have drowned.
Some of them have watched other children
drown over and over.

They walk to Coconut Plantation
or another nearby beach, let's say, in Sinkor
or Congo Town.

They will swim until the sun sets.
Maybe it is the tropical sunshine or the idleness
of oncoming youth

or something outside of something that gets them.
When Mammie Wata came out
that day, she was like a shadow

in the sun's rays, watching the swimming
children or watching the ocean
going up and down.

She stood in the middle as if on a rock
or on a pier or on something that holds up
only a Mammie Wata.
She was not white or black or brown,
I'd say, but her hair fell at her back, flying with
the ocean breeze even though

she'd just come out of the deep
or so it seemed to my eyes.
Look at that, I said when she flipped
like a fish on a fishtail.

One of the other children screamed, and everybody
stared, speechless.

She's really a fish, I thought, a woman-fish
or a fish-woman or a woman with
a fish at her tail, or a woman,

standing in the middle of the foamy ocean,
carrying a fish at her tail for feet.

"What are you talking about?"
Mama cried, when I told her.
"You didn't see Mammie Wata-eh,
my child, please, tell me, you didn't."

The Women in My Family

The women in my family were supposed
to be men. Heavy body men, brawny
arms and legs, thick muscular chests and the heart,

smaller than a speck of dirt.
They come ready with muscle arms and legs,
big feet, big hands, big bones,

a temper that's hot enough to start World War Three.
We pride our tiny strings of beards
under left chins as if we had anything

to do with creating ourselves.
The women outnumber the men
in the Jabbeh family, leaving our fathers roaming

wild nights in search of baby-spitting concubines
to save the family name.
It is an abomination when there are no boy children.

At the birth of each one of us girls, a father lay prostrate
on the earth, in sackcloth and ash, wailing.

It is an abomination when there are no men
in the family, when mothers can't
bring forth boy children in my clan.

For Ma Nmano Jabbeh: A Dirge

Hne Nmano, *Sagba-Nyene*, I come to you singing
long after you were gone. Your brown beauty
and sad laughter remain here forever.
I still see you standing there in the middle
of the house; your Grebo-English voice, like fire
in the March sunshine of tropical farm burning.
So when the rains come, rice farmers
will plant single rice grains in tiny holes
over acres of charcoal-ash ground.

In late February, the farmer dreads the coming
of early rains. They say we do not eat with the same
heaviness of heart we took to brush the farmland,
with which we felled the oak. How did you let
the war overwhelm you so? How could you let
the world speed you so early away in its swift winds?
The world, where you were the one that made
daylight come so quickly. My father was the king
only you could fashion with your soft,
swift palms under pungent spices.

Mother of mothers, the mother I could never have—
the one who could take a lone child in, and yet, leave
her sitting at the doorpost. I'm still singing dirges
for you, Sagba. I call on you to wake up because
day has broken through the fields.
The sun's rays have come penetrating the years,
and yet you sleep. I long again to see your
solemn complexity, your anger and your
fear of drawing too close to the stepdaughter.

I spread out lappas for you under the December
sky while the grass is still wet—lappas upon lappas
carpet my driveway while dawn comes in with fresh
dew upon my lawn, and at night, bats cannot hide

under the eaves of my roof of tarred shingles
in stranger land. How does a daughter lay out
The Mat just to wail alone? When our brothers put
The Mat down, mourners come

from far away towns, wailing for the Warrior
Woman's passing. It is the son that must put down
The Mat so the *Newordeh* will sit and wail.
So our brothers' wives, our *Bai-de* can show off
their sweet dirges in winding tones.
So our men can prove to us, *Newordeh*, their
manhood, and then under the burial tent, you can
hear the elders in their *Bati-oh-Bati*; proverbs,
rising out of ancestral lands.

Then from hut to hut, we spread out your lappas
from the years on the verandas. So the coming
mourners can come and see what a life
you once had. It is the kola nut then that welcomes
the stranger among us Kin.
But now, all your sons and our brothers
are gone before you. Where will Passersby learn
our town's history? Where will the women,
singing dirges to you, find a place
to stretch out and wail?

Hne Nmano, Townswoman, for whom men
will go to war. How is it you left before the town
could gather? Before the Town Crier was conceived
after the killing of the Town Crier?
I am the child who missed her way into
your possession, and sat in, even though you
did not want me. Did the war teach you at last
that the owl does not have to wail at the setting
of the sun before the sun sets?

The rooster crows only for its own coming day,
but we think it is for us that the rooster
flaps strong wings upon a tree stump to crow?
At the Springs Payne Airfield while the plane
waited, there you were, clinging to me, singing
a dirge for your own burial.
Sagba, the one that could take my leopard father
by the horns, and let him follow
wherever you went.

To a Mother, After Passing

Everything's different for you at your leaving.
People returned in groups, crowded in taxis, cars, or just
walking from the bus stop after the funeral.
Small groups now gather in fours, fives, and sevens.
There is black everywhere—

black dresses, bubbas, gowns, pants, coat suits,
hats, caps, neckties, even the cars are black.
The day is turning black slowly, cloudy.
Life has turned a little darker
since we let you into your new home.

Inside, the women wail loud—no one understands
your leaving. Some people eat after they
lay a body in the grave. Uninvited guests,
seated. They believe they will
be fed for coming to a funeral.

Pots clang, cups jingle—tea is passed around.
Tea? Why tea? I say, tea in this hot sun?
And after tea, one by one, the group leaves
in buses, cars, taxis…it's been
two long weeks with you dying

close to Flag Day, people have asked
to be fed Flag Day food. Outside,
the yard stands. Cold settles slowly upon
the stool you left at the doorway.
Even the stool now knows

you're gone. Your dogs used to bark at first,
when you'd just left, barking at noon,
at night, at dawn. Only a rooster's crow
could set the barking off until
the sun returned in the morning.

But now, the Shepherd sits wagging a tail,
staring. It is not just the Shepherd looking
on the road for you now...today,
your four-year-old sat upon
the stool, waiting.

For the Lucky Wife

She met her husband where Harper and Pleebo
highways merge, where trucks, loaded with bananas

and cassavas wait for a drink of gasoline. When Harper
was Harper, and a man was a man. When you could see

tomorrow in the twilight over the banana búshes
in your backyard. The Clan stuck the Rooster's Feather

in her hair then, with a bull, palm wine, and green cash.
The cattle she brought into the clan was bride price for

many more wives so the Tuobo Clansmen could live.
Tidi carried her youth on her body then—shining dark

arms, long eyelashes and hair. Today, one does not bring
a bride home by the horns of a bull—after many years,

her husband has forgotten. His eyes, darting this way
and that way, eyeballs, pale, as if he were looking for

a third woman to add to his new book woman. They take
the likes of Tidi's husband, put some sour-sap together

and whip it into his head, and he is drunk with book.
Tidi, the lucky wife, whose husband is a high court judge.

The lucky wife of a book-worm husband, the one hut
that was burnt before the forest fire reached the hut.

Tidi, daughter of *Bodior*, the high priest without whom
no one can get to God. Tidi, whose father wore the *Bodior*

bangle around his ankle, slept with it, made the ground stir,
wearing it; her father who lived such a life, they planted

a baobab at the head of his grave. Gbafor Tidi, Jeh-jeh,
warrior child, head wife, thunder woman. After all these

years why do you still sit at a market shed in Monrovia?
After so long, why are you still selling bitter balls and okra,

plantains and cassavas, peppers and snuff down Waterside?
Why are you sitting where the din of everyday hurries

the market woman to her grave? When August comes,
Tidi pulls a lappa over her head so rain water drains

down kindly. Then comes March, and she pulls her lappa
over her head to hold back the sun while her husband sits

in court, long black gown, banging the hammer, so the
man who does not feed his wife is handcuffed and jailed.

The wife's children will be fed from the handcuffed man's
confiscated paycheck. But the judge who abandons his

country-wife will keep banging the hammer, calling in new
cases, giving away his own paychecks to the woman with

the booky-head, the woman whose skirt pinches her legs
so tight everybody sighs when she passes. The *Kwii* one

who does not want to grow old. The Monrovia woman,
the one with the Mammie Wata hair, the needle-legged one.

Women at the Tomb

The women and the empty tomb,
a jar of alabaster oil and some tears
in case the oil isn't enough.
The two Marys and Salome—
they come rushing, pushing aside wet brush of dew
along the footpath at the outskirts of Jerusalem.
After three days, the corpse should now
smell like a corpse, they think.

It is Mary as usual, the other Mary, not Salome,
but the sly one, the Mary who knows how to cleanse
the Master's feet with just oil and hair.
The other Mary, the one who knows
how to sit still, holding on to the perfume oil,
she comes today with a soft towel to wipe
the Master's chilled feet.

Two days ago, did the storm knock over
the gravestone and did the dead rise?
Or did he push the stone all by himself?
Mary pushes the other Mary aside,
"Wait a minute," she sighs.
The tomb's big stone, the panting women
now sorry, the stone has been rolled
away, and the Master, gone.

Mary, her fingers examining the swaddling cloth,
as if the owner had vanished.
She screams, and running before the other
Mary has time to feel it all for herself.
Nothing is real until it becomes real,
she thinks. The other Mary
with the poking fingers picks up the cloth,
holding it, wide eyed.
How could the Master push

away a heavy stone, bleeding, and doing
it anyway, bare-foot, running into hiding,
or did someone lift him, holding him up
so he could walk on nail-pierced feet,
blood oozing out his sides
where the Roman guards had poked the spear—
or did he really rise into thin air, and if he
did, where did he go?

Poem Written from a Single Snapshot

On the beach in Monrovia,
my children and I are building sandcastles.
You can see the Atlantic's waves in the distance,
fighting for a place to roll their way onto shore.
Waves are flapping in the wind
as the tide rises up and down.
Before we know it, we are in the middle of water.
Besie is two years old. MT, who is only
six months, clings a short arm around my knee.
He's staring at Besie and the sandcastle
she's erecting with her right foot.
This is how my mother taught me
to build a sand castle.
You put your foot down
and build mounds around it until
the castle becomes stable.
This is how we search for home.
You put your foot down in a place long enough
that new place becomes home.

Broken World

To every winning team, many more will lose—
Many defenders, goalies, linebackers, dribblers, attackers,

ball catchers, and now one lone, winning cup from which
no one will ever drink. To every war, there are no winners.

To every living, many more dead will go unmarked.
So many lives lined up for death; so much of what took

forever to build, goes up in some cloud. So many buried
alive or executed—a stray bullet, accidentally passing.

So many players who never knew the name of the game
they played, yet they played, without even knowing they

were playing until someone found them dead by the road-
side. Today, here are St. Louis Rams, walking away from

the Super Bowl, carrying the Super Trophy. Tennessee
watches with a tearful eye. But below the deep Atlantic

in Abidjan, a plane has just gone down. One hundred
and sixty-nine, gone down, and all this time, I was here

watching what Americans call *Super Bowl*. I do not know
the game; it is not even my game to lose or win, but my

heart pounds hard for the game. Sometimes, I can feel
my skin slowly becoming American. Is life a game you can

win or lose? Will winning warlords ever know the extent
to which they have lost their war? How can anyone count

those who have won and those who have lost our war?
How can anyone travel from town to town, from country

to country, from refugee camp to refugee camp, counting
our living? How could we dig up each shallow mass grave

for all the tens of thousands who were never counted?
Why should anyone want to count at all? Show me the trophies

of our war, so I will take you to a field, where all
the massacred still gather at night to bind open, bullet

wounds even though they are already dead. When warriors
come home from war, carrying on their hands trophies

of booty, all the bullets from their weapons, gone, do
we ask them to show us their scars? The after-war Dorklor,

with all its drumming and dancing, was never meant
to be merry—not even in their jubilation at victory.

You have only to watch the dancing warriors' feet to know.

Design and Production

Cover and text design by Kathy Boykowycz

Text set in Stone Serif, designed in 1987 by Sumner Stone
Title set in Univers 67, designed in 1957 by Adrian Frutiger
Main title set in Pompeia Inline, designed in 1997 by
   Victor de Castro

Printed by Thomson-Shore of Dexter, Michigan,
on Nature's Natural, a 50% recycled paper